MARY O'MALLEY was born in Connemara in 1954 and educated at
University College, Galway. She travels and lectures widely in
Europe and America, has written for both radio and television and is
frequent broadcaster. She has been an organiser for the Cuirt
festival and a member of the council of Poetry Ireland, and is a
member of Aosdána. She teaches on the MA in Writing at the
National University of Ireland, Galway. Mary O'Malley's earlier
collections *Where the Rocks Float* (1993), *The Knife in the Wave* (1997)
and *Asylum Road* (2001) were published by Salmon Poetry. *The
Boning Hall* was published by Carcanet in 2002, and a selection of her
poems was included in Eavan Boland's anthology *Three Irish Poets*,
published by Carcanet in 2002.

D1392068

The Boning Hall

MARY O'MALLEY

A Perfect V

CARCANET

First published in Great Britain in 2006 by
Carcanet Press Limited
Alliance House
Cross Street
Manchester M2 7AQ

A CIP catalogue record for this book is available from the British Library
ISBN 1 85754 839 6
978 1 85754 839 6

The publisher acknowledges financial assistance from Arts Council England

Typeset by XL Publishing Services, Tiverton
Printed and bound in England by SRP Ltd, Exeter

Acknowledgements

Acknowledgements are due to the *Irish Times*, *PN Review* and *Something Beginning with P: New Poems from Irish Poets* (O'Brien Press, 2005), in which some of these poems first appeared.

Thanks to the Centre Culturel Irlandais in Paris where several of the poems were written, and to the archivists of the Special Collections Room at NUIG library.

Contents

Silence

for Michael Longley

A word, one syllable only
like love or death. Now
it is moving closer, it's dynamo charged,
into this orbit
the ice still on its skin.

It's surface – surely it is a sphere –
hums faintly
keeping its distance.

I am its sun.
It is my traitor moon.

My skin is bruised from surfaces colliding.
There is nowhere to run except the edge
of the roof, the tip of the wing.

It watches me climb down and like God
makes no protective move
nor does it show its bright or darkened face.

It waits. It has been waiting since the first sentient life
in the universe
to make contact again.

It is the third person singular of the verb to be
is, becoming,
like an iced red berry ripening.

Condensing on my parched face
September rain.

My House Is Not For Sale

Nor is my life. I have moved away
to another hill and will stay
as long as the gods allow.
My house was built of love and blue

and bits of hope, snagged on the furze,
it's true, but, little harpy, get your fuchsia talons
off the mast. Watch out for falcons.
My ark floats high over Orbsen's lake.

It waits for the day when foxes and panthers
entering two by two, will cock their ears
at song returning. It is anchored in my bedrock –
it waits for me and for some dark

bridegroom to light a fire over the waters
and, warm again, take stock of where we are.

The Heart

In the world's share I have been given houses.
Why do we trust them
when their passages and doors
shift, leaving us staring at blank walls,
tottering on the landing
of a demolished staircase?

Houses are fragile. Those built
of concrete blocks, the marriage shelters,
are worst. There is too much hope
in their dreaming, too little mortar.
The heart too, with it's rusting atrium.

The Time When I Was Not

for C.B.

Small wars were starting.
You phoned and said, *Howya?*
Big wars were starting, wild strawberries
were spreading by the roadside, unpicked
because you do not eat the fruit from that time.
Blood was splashing the shopfronts of desert countries.
You called: *Now you will start to accept.*

They sent pictures from Titan. A poet from America
described an idiot walking in the Manhattan traffic,
an explanation of Ireland came apart in my hands.
This was for my daughter, my son
but the words lifted like leaves.
You said: *Now you'll begin to remember yourself.*

The time when I was not, God juggled a baby
in the rush hour traffic and a voice
that could have been mine called *Please.*
Please. The idiot turned and smiled
his idiot smile. He threw the child high,
let his hands hang down, shrugged
and caught it at the last second.
The poet said: *That's God, the idiot.*

The time when I was not
my grandmother's house was bulldozed into the river.
You said: *Now? Now you'll become autonomous.*

The pictures from Titan were like snaps
of somewhere I had been and had a good time.
Time itself is camera obscura.
There is a woman. She cries, washes clothes.
A panther stalks. A hawk's panoptic eye
shoots stills of her life
but makes no sense of it, no
and no one has to fill in the blanks.

You showed me a blue floor.
You sent a text: *Salix babylonica pendula,*
I think. Why?

Because willow if it grows will weep
tears of fresh green
over my gate when the soul
or whatever bright thing comes
slowly towards us from the plains
telling that wolves menace the night
singing of snow and crevices and ice

when the soul, or some shining thing
that resembles the soul
returns and enters my dry husk.

The Miracle of the Cherry Tree

Where is home now?
The sleeping child is grown,
the men are gone
about their business in the town.
When the journey ends
the hearth is cold.

Separation

No. Love should not end like this.
A box of tissues, a dotted page.
Sorry. Everyone finds it hard.
Sign here. The back of our marriage
certificate is white. On my left hand
the gold mark of your absent wedding band
comes up like invisible ink as I unwrite
my name, reversing the vow. Shame rises
in a tidal blackout. X is innocent. Cunning
life has us outfoxed. I sign the forms,
consenting to our surgical untwinning.
In another room you are doing the same

with a cheap pen, across a scratched desk.
Where is the photographer, the ludicrous cake?

December 2004

Those cats' paws on the water
were the start of a hurricane year.
It raged through our solstices,
drawing the last blue
into the sleeve of its own dark interior.
It turned the world inside out.

Tonight the wave of luck
runs high in Silverhill.
It laps the bedroom floor.
I kneel to it. *Drown the old year.*
Suck it under. Burn it.
Freeze it. Turn it.

On Friars' Hill

When you set out for Ithaca
Pray that your journey be long...
                                        Cavafy

This late at night household objects
are no longer inert or friendly,
they send out ashy emanations.
The cold TV, the stained glass panel
and the telephone tremble slightly
in their thingy dreams.

Almost eighteen years ago
we came back from the sun
with two young children
to this, our university town.
Here, unknown to us,
a street was being laid down.

On the opposite hill
two horses grazed, Summer and Winter
much loved by our small daughter.

High in the constellations
trajectories of burning stars
were converging. Despite
projections of disaster
each collision was avoided.

When I came home tonight
the cats flowed towards me,
a street-lit cloud, a grey shadow.

Home? There is no danger of elegy.
We will never be thirty years married now.
The wedding ring
that is our gold O of delight
and 'forever' and sits
in a dark drawer, still fits.
When we set out for Ithaca
with glowing faces I gave you youth

and fire as well as grief.
Although this barren island
was not the expected destination,
we acquired amber and ebony
and our journey was long.

The horses have gone,
replaced by houses.
On every street, in every new estate,
it is starting again.

This November night
there is a moon
caught in a fine mesh
of mist. It comforts me to know
I could walk up that opposite hill
where the white mare and brown horse were
and the bay would spread out
west, to water and escape.

The Psychoanalysis of Fire

after Bachelard

Last night I dreamed my house
was burning. It had moved west
to be with my body. It had settled
in a fold on the coast of possibility

near Horse Island. It looked well there
but it was burning and only the salt water
could quench it. Either the house was too far inland
or the sea couldn't reach it. In the dream

the roof collapsed, sparks hanging,
hanging then drifting down like medusa's tendrils.
The windows exploded and what woke me
was how my right arm hurt when they held me back

and the flames, drooping in the warm daylight.
Even in the dream I knew my house was empty,
but I wanted the vase of harebells we pick
from our necessary strand for their flat blue music

because always, on every table
they are the foreground of the waves.

Differences

Marriage makes love familial.
There is tedium, bitching, care
but there are also children.
I do not believe we failed in general.
Ours was held together like the universe
with string and theory and a slab foundation.
Between the cutlery and schoolbooks
when physics wanders into biology,
it all comes down to absolutes and relativity.

The Shannon Stopover

The next house will be bone,
a cruciform scrimshaw my passport.
There will be a red lamp by the door

in a niche. They will sit, the gateposts
on the highwater mark
in spring and all the solstices.

Welcome to life in the metal hum
of gated love, the votive glow of blood
flowing through the atrium.

Here, it is pitch black behind the mask,
a surprisingly soft hood
Though my wrists chaff, blisters burst.

I won't think of the electrodes
until it happens. Yesterday someone
lifted the hood. A place with shades

of green out of a Hollywood film,
Ireland of the welcomes,
the colour of Islam. My English comes

back to me in clichés. Bright
floating things whirl around my head,
explode, blowballs of white light,

and the unbearable green world
refuses me. I am spared leprechauns.
Who knows what the drugs and the dark hoard.

The terrible, the ridiculous. A bush –
bush! – flowers white, bridal. Each blossom tiny.
The hood drops its deep kiss.

Every breath is torture. If you cry
the cloth sucks a cave mouth,
a black comfort blanket. Slow. Easy.

In. Out. In. Out. Show the heart. Ruth says
my name. My real name. Cat's tongue rough,
her voice is here, her hand, please

just once let me be mad enough
to feel it where the noose chafes
my neck. I know the photographs

of uniformed women. Could I survive
being little Lyndie's dog? The mad children
picking the legs off flies, the balls off captives?

Fruit or insects: it comes screaming one night
the truth – they do not know we are human.
A year in Guantanamo and they'll be right.

This is interactive television,
the media game. The truth is nothing
has happened that has not been seen.

I am not here unless a camera scans
this patch of Ireland, unless the light seeks this jet,
lances its metal womb and reveals

my curled shape, my minotaur's head.
I want to be born again here, before
they fly me to Never Never Land.

They lift the hood for me to drink. A sign
dances. The wire cuts all but *Mile. Fail*
-te. I stretch but there is nothing

more. The engines hum. Tears wet
my cheeks. My cheeks. I see
sandy coloured soldiers, Christ's

desert booted army stream like ants
across the tarmac. This is America.
The darkened mind plays tricks. I thought

I heard a woman singing low and sweet:
I saw the heron dip his Parthian red beak at Kells;
no matter what verses or prayers I recite

that bright bush gleams like silver coins
in the hooded dusk. The engines thrust.
My head is pushed between my knees.

Give me citizenship of this planet –
at least one witness to speak for me
here at the perimeter fence. *Vos papiers?* Poet?

Riddle

There was no one to dip me into Lethe's water
and make me impermeable.
I sit in the black boat's bow, tending a bucket of fire.
From here, the land is a few clean strokes, manageable.

There is oil on the water, burkas sail past,
sailboat blue or black, the women's crescent eyes
cut you. False lashes hover over the surface.
Lipstick and a sword tip draw blood. Silk cut.

Look down into the woods, the ships, the steeplejacks
ascending into wonder, up two flaming towers.

The priests in the city they ask it of me
How many strawberries grow in the salt sea
I answer them back with a tear in my eye
How many planes fly in the forest?

St John's Eve

In the blue light that lets us see
my husband's shirt buttons on bonfire night
and see our mink-coated dog
in the distance at half eleven at night,
a butterfly wings in from Borneo. It is the colour
of luminous blue fish in an aquarium.

It drinks our attention until the lavender hills,
the silver hound leaping for a tennis ball,
the girl throwing it, sixteen and beautiful,
become a film, a vacuumed surface.
We watch this creature visiting from space,
from heaven, from somewhere else, transfixed.

Go back, I want to say. *You are in the wrong place.*
It hovers for a while, pulsing blue light,
then flies off towards the coast.
We stare, robbed of a dimension. I am afraid.
I ask God what sacrifice would be enough
to keep us all together. I am talking to a stranger.

Naturalists write neater poems than lovers.
I would have promised anything.
All I observed besides the fire blossoming
below the house was a brown O on each wing.
I could taste the shining bone that would remain
a charred promise in the morning ashes.

Madonna Drowning

Within the year, it will all be over,
her lovely life gone and longed for
like the blue winged thing she feared,
and uselessly as Medea crying
for all she has killed. Afterwards
the thing she feared will happen:

people she never saw will say they knew her secrets.
This is why when she dives, she'll take her pearls.

Men

O Nora did you really say
To macho Ernest Hemingway
Boasting of his skill with gun and dagger
I wish my Jim could meet a tiger.

James Joyce Impersonates Pessoa

I am plural. I know and relish this.
Heteronyms live in me – Alberto Caeiro
is master. Others make do with an alter ego.
I have multitudes, a rush of voices
jumping upriver – Anna Livia Plurabelle.
Some don't make it. One of these days
I'll finish my long book
set in Lisbon on the eighth of March.
That'll make them sit up.
One of the others can get on with *Dubliners*.

There are nights I am afraid to sleep
for fear of Alvaro's dreams.
I am not mad, only short-sighted.
Ophelia Barnacle Queiroz,
where did I leave my glasses?

Chinese Whispers

After

Under the hawthorn tree of your lover
when the first September moon
rises behind the house
you'll be able to dream
if your lover hasn't gone
and the gods are benign
the dreams of another.

Communion at the Gate Theatre

This is the time of life when a woman
goes to Dublin to the theatre to get away
the night every Leaving Cert student in Ireland
is up from the country to see the same RSC production.

Hamlet is small and elegant and very English. What did
she expect – that after all those years
he would have grown really Danish, the lies
would be less eloquent, gestures less fluid?

Tonight she finds the prince tedious and self-obsessed.
You are thirty years old for Christ's sake,
she shouts, startling the audience.
The students are disapproving, then delighted.

Now that they have stopped texting one another,
the girls are shaping some of the words.
There is Royal Shakespearean body language
between Claudius and Gertrude.

The boys whistle, applaud uneasily.
The woman thinks Gertrude is entitled to her lover's kiss.
What kind of twisted little shit are you?
she asks Hamlet, but silently. Hamlet is relentless.

The actor fifty if he's a day, torturing his mother
who is the same age. No one cares.
It's as bad as MacLiammoir playing Romeo.
The kids are loving it. *We are rearing*

a generation of throwbacks, she thinks,
without Latin to sustain them, much less history.
She checks the exits, measures her chances. She rises
in a crouch just as a hush is spreading through the house.

Here and there along the rows the students begin
to mouth Hamlet's soliloquy. The half-formed faces
half-lit are devout. At *What is a man if his chief good be…*
but to sleep… the ungodly voices join in as at Mass.

Ixion Stopped

Tony McMahon Plays Raglan Road

And every girl pregnant with disappointment
and death is in it. The man on the rock
saying, *is uaigneach a bheith fireann*
ar an gcarraig crua seo, is in it. It is played
on the ribcage, teased out of the bone nest
of the tune with care, with skill. Kept beating –
for the exact caesura a tired heart needs.
Then resumes.

I have heard it fleshed out with lush curves,
too much pigment in the tint. This is the poem
scored on bone, the tune given back to itself.
The stops played this way once, and only once.
The air shivers. Her own dark hair
a glint of copper – the snare. The sign that's known.

is uaigneach a bheith fireann / ar an gcarraig crua seo: 'It's lonely to be a
man on this hard rock'.

The Well Below the Valley

To turn into the year's gyre,
the plough blade, the slow morning radio grind
of a winter world you cannot face
without protection, circle the stone dial
seven times, the well. In your cold feet,
raw boned, berry stained, ask for sweet
tea afterwards for shock.

Here, no growth dies back.
There are no surprises. We buried
what we did not want seen.
And if you dig, expect bone shards.
Expect stab wounds
and the tiny delicate spines
of the fruit of violation. Expect no mercy.

The De Danann Tapestries

for Alec at sixty

Who would unstitch a tune from its haunting, unpick
the cross hatching of those instruments –
silk from the fiddle, chain mail, a medieval slub:
the bucks, the boys, the soloists' embroidery.

Maura's voice darting silver between the musicians'
fingers, sewed a river flowing against
the stretched air – fiddle fast, steady drum when time
obeyed unholy orders, rin tin whistle, ran tan bodhran.

Now the hunt is on for the king's own prey. Rust-edged notes
draw blood – Delores. Stooked downstage she threaded
blue ribbons through the foreign innovations. And all agreed
sweet mandolin, they were continental occasions.

You could hear a pin drop, afterwards, in slow motion
and the feathery silence of the homing falcon.

The Change

This, then must be the thick of it,
our time of change, the wombs baying, the night
stretched thin. The light strokes of time,
daybreak, evening, the seams
between seasons are smudged and basted
where the sixth sense, her nutmeg eyes, the second
sight, shone in and lasered pain away.

This Good Friday the soul does not know
itself, having no mirror to reflect
its long eclipse, nor the promise of a fingerclip
moon. This is the bitch moon's last betrayal.
Mars and Saturn refuse to cool
the furnace stoked by cursing Alexanders
and all the Hecubas cry their iron tears.

Suicide

The full moon rides along the rim
of November strand and desert.
Two falcons scythe it into crescents
that grin – watermelon slices
bled white along the edges.

When he left she picked cowrie shells
and two late cornflowers
the inferior blue of cheap sapphire,
crushed eyes, the colour
leached into the sky.
In summer, daylight's reverse,
the blue is gentian glorious.
She'd have held the jesses
forever. He loosed them
and the barking curses.

Felix Redivivus

The tiger came back last night. Stayed
lost so long black pillow talk crackled,
then just walked in, stalked the table, lay down.
His green gunsight eyes licked the room.
Click, action. On the rim
of the dream-pit, flame rippled.

Whiteout at Five a.m.

i.m. John Borrowman

Just after dark the lights go out.
The transformer has blown or been shot.
Men in insect shoes are climbing poles
invisibly, a flying saucer or
high flying car is sweeping headlights
along the whispering beauty of trees
made sibilant by rain. When I wake at five a.m.
a student is dancing down the street
looking for another party, singing
of all things *Swing low, sweet chariot.*

The master switch snaps down and shocks the sleepers
who left lamps, TVs, cookers on. The street wakes
to mayhem and the boy below the window dances,
arms raised in thanks for his first miracle
...coming for to carry me hooome,
his scarecrow coat, his flapping wings.
The spit of you, down to the grin.

Arrival in Paris

Fluent gesture. Already on the Beauvais bus a man
strokes his son's head with palm cupped.
The child's black hair responds like a young cat.

A boy is sulking beautifully,
legs crossed at the ankles. The girl
ignoring him is reading Kafka – *La Procès*.
He utters soft plosives, little plumes of indignation
astonished at her cruelty for at least ten kilometres.
When they make up, she rubs the side of his face
with slow fingers for another five before he defrosts.

There are banks of hawthorn along the motorway.
By Paris, the lovers are reconciled. Outside
open-pored sandstone drinks in the south.
I think of Blaithin, her skin made of flowers,
the touch of sun opening them.

Libra

In the blockhouse Pantheon a brass ball swings
making an elegant arc in clear strokes.
This is the world made simple enough to save our lives.
A few curves, circles,
arcs that intersect or don't and the marks
of a clean universe centre on a brass disc, a dome,
a faintly astrological suggestion in coded stone.

Behind it, a medieval Christ gives his last
judgement in a glass panel of violent red.
His knee is bare, his hunter's torso half exposed.
He is flanked by the Virgin and St John.
By this juxtaposition of sweet reason
with a just and savage retribution of flesh
and fire, France mocks it's own refinement.

With each swing the red-robed God appears again,
undaunted by science's shining pendulum
which never falters in its reasoned swing.

On Rue Des Irlandais

There should be funerals, clay, the tamp of spades.
After the tea, brown bread, people talking about fridges

there should be empty fortifying condolences.
Well, I never expected roses, they want you to say.
It could have been worse, but there's no body,
just a shawl slipped from your shoulders.

There should be a year of mourning, a black diamond.
Then the first Sunday after it ends, new clothes,
a dance. These days God denies everything.
You have to put yourself together again, like crochet

with bits of Lisbon, purgatory, New York in a mosaic of complaints.
Tastes – feta, cherries, tincture of Armagnac help
but make no sense. It could be worse. I have found sanctuary.
This city, composed of a million single people in attics

grieves enjoyably. It is twelve o' clock. All's well. Echoes
of prayer and the ghosts of sacraments
lap around my feet, communion, matrimony,
absolution. We are safe. There is a night watchman.

The Jack of Hearts

So it's over. Again. How dare you agree.
I want you to feel me close and think *Christ*...
and beg. I want to slam the door in your face.
Not metaphorically, Mr Objective Co-Relative,
oak. I want you
to feel the slip of my nightdress that isn't there
under your fingers and hear the midnight
laughing on the phone when I'm kicking your absence.

So you're with another love already. Isn't there
a prescribed period of mourning, like a week.
She's kind to you and never loses her temper.
A saint. You're blissfully happy and content
in a sleeping bag on the dunes. In Wales.
Darling, I'm in Paris in a skirt and heels.
We disagreed over hills, remember?
She must be ecstatic (what else can go with kiss)
Over all those places with sheep, a prince and double ells.
You'll be sure to fill her in on all those deserted Protestant chapels.

I've re-read your letter. Thank you for telling me
so immediately and in such detail about the bliss,
soft rain and making love to the sound of the sea.
You can see how I had to check it wasn't a filmscript
with the happy ending and all those mauve adjectives.

I'm glad she's supplied the missing bits of you, that the fit
is perfect. Pity about your prose, once taut, alive.
Your literary style is slipping and the slip is showing.
Next time try a telegram. You're glad I'm spoilt?
I'm thrilled you're thrilled. Goodbye

First Confession

And I have never gone to the asylum,
lacking courage, having children.
I have two tribes. One will never forgive.

I have not unpicked the marriage blanket
Nor untangled the clotted rivers.
I have kept them running
These three years, four years, though tired.

And besides where I come from
Death has no fascination.
We know its purple face.

We know how long it takes
for the corpse to rise
and what becomes of the eyes,
the impenetrable lapis.

Statues breathe on her,
paintings sound deep green notes.
Red booms in her ears.

The Stations of the Cross march
fourteen times Christ's suffering eyes.
When it was good there was
a rose on her pillow, the scent

of sainthood, the stitches fine and close.
On bad mornings the seams
of the sky parted, her dog-toothed stitches
leaving home in shame, letting the world down.

The day I felt like dying
no one was playing the fiddle
the bookshop in Paris was musty.

The young woman was writing
a note for the babysitter,
instructions for the doctor.
Nobody wants to be dead.

Only the high church steeples
that might be carved from light's opposite
held me above love's going, the terrible precipice.

That's what she told herself, but who is to know
the true measure of such moments –
like pitting lust against the moon.

Paris Nocturne

Collège des Irlandais

At Shakespeare and Company
the beautiful young women are hopeless
at books but talk eruditely about lovers.
The shop crawls with lice and destiny.

Bob Dylan walks in and asks
For Italian poems from the fifteenth century.
He withers under the glassy stare.
Perhaps over there. With the poetry,

the blonde says, meaning *Aren't you too old?*
I am reading Sylvia's last letters, confronted
with the gap between words and the pit,
when in waltzes Marina to the rescue, the spit

of some movie Electra in sunglasses,
glides right through the gloom and we're off,
walking up the Boul' Mich' in high heels just
like grown women, Bob. We laugh

at the bad boys' diaries and sex and Shakespeare,
and talk about Artaud on Inis Mór, how the weather
will drive us all mad. A light blue sports car
fins past – hey Lucy Jordan, you should have

stuck it out until forty-seven, a decade's penance
and you could have had Paris, the evening sun,
the sports car. What harm would the wait have done?
Dylan, bookless, walks by. *Wrong song, sisters.*

We toasted a blue moon sailing
through the glass ceiling of Saint Chapelle,
and the ghosts of a century of priests
that jumped over the College wall,

found revolution, books and women.
Later in the courtyard, two homesick mothers
we cried, yes Bob, just like little girls
for those redeemed and sent back shriven.

The News from Titan

after Chegal

Nitrogen might reveal the secrets of the universe.
We would welcome a sea of tar, blood even.
Something liquid. Of course there will be more probes
but already it is looking good, if barren.

We will soon know how they got on:
goat, fiddle, equestrian. Perhaps
this is where the beautiful bandits go,
the ones who don't make it down in Mexico.

Let us suppose our governments are lying,
there is no interior, no need
for all those expensive expeditions,
no fabulous stone city in the hills.

What if the Titans are flourishing,
the sea is blue, with properties of eternal youth,
magnificent fish, and those pictures they sent back
are just elaborate jokes?

What if there are gambling dens, *federales*
On the take and under the gorgeous surface
Of the moon, the swarming slaves?

Cocteau in Antibes

The poet's eye is always open.
When asleep
he walks with false eyes,
wide, blinded,
down the storm wall. To his left
the sphinx
flaps her soft white wings.

Above her woman's breasts
her face
is unlined. *Look*, I want to shout,
take those false
eyes out and wake up. Stop
feeling your way.
But he won't risk seeing her, the riddle
failing the test

And the rocks below
and the crystal sea.

Sunday Morning at Le Baron Rouge

He is waiting by the door, two wine glasses
placed on the timber cask. Compact.
He doesn't take a single sip: it is hot.
Tiny droplets mist both glasses.

When she breezes in he touches her face
with joy, her body arches back, leans
into him. With a small camera he snaps
her cheek, her smile, her eyes in close-up.

Now they sip the rough wine. His hand slides
down her side and lightly squeezes her hip.
This will be a slow devouring. You wish them luck
and afterwards, as well as can be expected.

In a café in Lisbon before love had broken camp –
your glasses left wet rings on the wood –
his hand on your hip, like them – snap. These streets –
click – saw resistance in the war, were rebuilt.

The café buzzes. You sit on a plastic chair
alone with your twist of flowers.
They gather their frivolous purchases.
Outside, the hot concrete stretches for hours.

Orison, St Gervais

Praise the light.
Praise the Gold Virgin,
the icon of beautiful Christ.
Rows of white-robed nuns sing to his beauty.
The girl in jeans sings, the man on the steps
bows his head between sips.
In Paris every church is allowed its beggar.
Praise the candle's gutter and the blaze of Babel
tracing a gold finger – some say it cruder –
into the night sky. Praise good coffee, white wine
dry as the bones in an ossiary.

Praise the cool air that seeps tonight into this café
on Rue Mouffetard where we talk of friends
and what matters in the end: love, children, work,
being alive now, how the old gods emigrate,
how they come back for a look. Crom Dubh
will scatter the posers, the critics,
the Kulture Kritters, the government.
We give Kavanagh, his moment and laugh.
Beckett is inevitable. After the rant, the begats.

Today I give praise
for night, the choice of mosque or synagogue or mass,
the nun playing the bull fiddle before an altar.
Call, answer. I went out for coffee and was brought
to this vaulted church.
A congregation drawn out of the city's capillaries
sings the psalms.
The songs are held in the ceiling's high curves
like the canted limbs of lovers
moving to their bodies' most eloquent conclusion.
Praise the word. When the splintered God will not visit
the word is gold.

Birthday Poem 2003

for Oisin

He can't be dealing with words.
They let you down
one way and another,
so he dreams himself back to a boat.
He lies tucked inside it, snug as a nut,
his face pressed close to the canvas. The ribs
mark his belly and his hand curls
around the rowel pin.
It is made from the *crann troim*,
a sacred poison tree that
hollowed to a blow pipe
gave our hills their name.
Na Beanna Beola – lips that blow
poisoned darts, people that whittle the bark.
A kind of poetry in that:
curses made flesh.

Silence in such places is blessed,
but no boat would sail
without this tree's protection.

We start again
with the old instructions:
first build a boat. *No*, he says,
first catch your tree.

Blue Willow

for Christian McCann

By the moongate in Denis's garden
the tangerine fishes blow bubbly kisses.
The young pearl fisher dives in to pick them.
They turn to moon opals – a necklace of wishes
for his princess.

Over there under the monkey-puzzle tree
there's a unicorn, sitting pretty –
exactly like the famous tapestry in France.
He has his silly eye on you but don't worry,
he's a bit of a prancy dancer.

Now your tiger with his stripes on fire is rippling
through the moongate in Denis's garden.
Cool cool fiery cat, close your eyes and fancy that
by the silvery zip-zapping scissory rip-rapping
only pretending-to-sleep napping sea.

Holding Rosa

The body does not long to be unencumbered.
The arm wants a child to hold away
from the boiling pot. I miss it: their fury
strident as junior paramilitaries,
their extravagant grievances, their bottomless sleep.
Mostly I miss their small bodies,
sweet as summer ices, as berries.

We can be parted from the sea and live.
It is like overcoming a stammer, or a tick.
By daily teaching the body new habits,
planets are persuaded out of orbit.

In seconds it is all undone. Holding Rosa
in a Dublin hotel is going to sleep
in a house on the shore and waking up
to the same sound. The magnetic dock
of child to hip, earth to moon, time stolen.

Rescue

I met Blue at the corner.
He watched the comings and goings
with cornerboy eyes. Over

the sunglasses, a light skin of ice.
Diamond blue, the aurora
good poteen gives when set alight.

That colour lifts the blood, makes men mad.
It enters the pores. A girl sailed along,
encased in jeans. He moved.

Her hair, vogue cut, was blue black.
She waltzed by laughing
with her brother. The sea played smack

into his hands. After the rescue she said,
We had fifteen minutes, and opening her arms
Pointed west to east. *The sun was half sunk*

when the helicopter came. We were swamped,
and shook with cold. I was glad to see you
on the quay. Blue darkened,

laid a hand on my neck. The night froze,
thawed. He slipped away between water and land.
The colour of the world changes three times:

when a child is born, when a parent dies and once
when a hand reaches down and out of all
the doomed sons and daughters, snatches up yours.

Surfing

for Oisin

Yesterday at seven o' clock a triangle of sky
between the asphalt, the Marine Science Building
and lush July trees took wing. It filled with the din
of young swallows, twittering weapons

flung on the increased air, making space liquid.
They scissor out of nowhere, junior jet pilots
not crashing once. This is a slice of day cut by Magritte.
The cubists deny there is a vanishing point.

This expanding envelope supports them.
The clean sky is threatened. Nearby a tree
planted in memory of a boy calls this wonder fragile.
Who was he? I think of his brief grace, his early fall.

At last you phone. Gone surfing with your friends,
black and swooping as those swallows
skating the glass slope of a wave
between dark and dark in this diamond of time.

Aillbrack Georgics

Plant something where the sun reaches,
shield the seedlings from the wind,
and grown, they will shelter you
and mark the edge of the storm.

If your nature is the salt ridge,
reap the wind, on the spring tide,
harness the white island horses
and plough the rocks under a full moon.

Gardening

Healing, yes. At a certain age, opera and clay
so you give in one spring day and buy bulbs,
seeds, poison for slugs, though what did slugs
ever do to you, and would it not make more sense
to buy pellets for the man whose absence
spreads like weeds, or even buy a man who knows
weeds from incipient flowers?

Grow things, they advise, *it'll do you good*,
and they talk long lists of Latin plants like odes.
Listen, you say, *I don't want the botanical dictionary,
just red and blue flowers.* So tell me
where to put the blood red roses,
who to sort out the briars, the tar baby
and the wind murdering the delphiniums.

Lynch

I

It was this James that gott his own son hanged
out of one of the windowes of his house
for having committed murther and broaken trust
towards a strange, for to be an example of sincere fidelity
for all posterity.

Five centuries on, the students milling outside the library text
and flirt. In this town where the versions were written.
They were this age when it happened. Agnes. Walter. Gomez.

Ireland, the notion of it, had just begun. The burghers'
loyalty is to the foreign queen and this her bastion;
the language, Shakespeare's with rougher diction
put this down in the minutes of the corporation,

much of whose business, then as now, was business –
licences granted, contracts for walls to be extended
before the plaintiffs, shivering like whitebait were dispensed

to gaol or fined. Crime – the papers are full of it
concerning butter, the price of it, salt, the sale of it
native dress, which must not be sold to the Irish,
and *no preste, monke nor frere* should keep a whore.

Across Ireland fortresses were growing like stalactites,
walls rammed into the resisting rock. Limestone
is softer, smudges blue. Its calcified embroidery reads
like a script of what will happen, given time.

What's time to a politician? Tacked to a capricious century
like all his Norman ilk with all his Norman
love of stone, to grow rich Lynch became England's toady.

And went too far. *Human nature sickens at such extreme justice.*
The story goes that a young Spaniard, one Gomez,
was a guest of the mayor, a friend of his son Walter.
Who loved Agnes. They were high spirited, like kids everywhere.

Gomez, this being a merchant's town, was friends
with her family and maybe because of his Spanish
manner, Agnes favoured him. Walter was jealous

and murdered his rival in a crime of passion.
This version did not come to rest by accident.
The window where the father hanged his son
was intentionally dragged from its context

and placed in the marketplace, or the market
was sited near the window, a façade
with no purpose but to advertise justice gone mad.

Let's clear something up. It wasn't over money
or the girl that Lynch the Mayor made history.
He is remembered for the sin of rigour. Perhaps
the men of the corporation could hear the death

rattle of their own relations next. In the other version –
Walter squandered his father's money on fun in Spain
and threw the merchant's nephew overboard.

Was it all about trade? They say crowds stopped
Lynch using the gallows so he did the job or had it done
at home – where it started. For this justice
he outlawed brightness, which comes from the sea

the hills outside. It could be those without
will find better cities to aim for or will die.
They could do better. They can do no worse.

Divorced from its hinterland, the town inside the walls
prospers. Wheels turn within wheels. One will refuse
to take the oath and be *putte oute* but no disgrace
will attach to that in a city under King's licence.

Outside the walls the native Irish swagger and strut
in the bogs, along the coast, in ships, avoiding taxes.
They live on berries, superstition and fish. They jut.

II

There was a girl. Inside the map, that round world staked
out for government, the ungovernable entered like a fast river.
Because we long for what is foreign, Gomez enters
bearing a tin tray of orange suns. Events happen.

When I trace the brown letters of *Liber A*, the dry
words of statutes, the agreed formulae, it is the girl I see,
the Spaniard leaving a house in Court Lane, the boy
doing his work with the dagger. In another library

in Atlanta, Georgia, postcards are on display, with captions
black bodies after the mob had finished with them. Lynched.
There is a clench of recognition.

Language has a diamond core. A polite black man
asks where I am from. *Ireland*, I say, *the South*,
and stare at the awful embodiment, thinking how a word
can make its way in spite of history to such a crooked truth.

The Road to Brightcity

Trust me. If you slide down the deep cuts
in the limestone apron on the way to the black fort
you will reach the colour red, you will reach
fire incarnate. Plenty from this island
have fallen through the cracks between Hell's Kitchen
and the Empire State. They hang in the air between
here and there. The tiny crimson tongues of songbirds
sing their Brightcity anthem in the December snow:

I see said the blind man
A hole in the wall
You're a liar said the deaf man
You can't see at all.

They wring no meaning from the earth
only music from stone, only water from bone
an oar, a Cadillac, the visa for home.

Untitled

We believe a person leaves some trace,
the slave, the sandhog, the prostitute from Ireland
unidentified in the city morgue.
What good to her is the mind's cold elegy,
the pen's fluency? Give her a tune.
Let her enter herself through the curtain parted
by music. The hands playing the fiddle lead back
like fingers dealing a pack of cards
to a hand that touched the waist of a woman
whose brother danced with her
in Calliope House. Someone always remembers
the name, the green flash of a dress,
islands on the way to a tune's origin.

Poem of the Sky

She inhabits space that was once empty,
convent air, agitated, then left.
She asks: *Where is he walking now?*
Between these four walls
and the sky the air is heavy
that between us, shared,
was light. In each room's cubed radiance
our thoughts collided like dancers.

What does her lover say of the waltzing,
the jiving? That she loved violets and ravens,
their conversation with the sky.

Love – An Explanation

Imagine there has always been a set of sympathetic strings
under your song. They have made the obvious atonal sounds of hills,
caves, distant pips quavering down into your low fathoms.
(They may even have been the seal's highwire cry.)

You follow them – what else? – blindly, up life's sharps
into marvellous light, into symphony. You learn to use
vestigial strings. Then you see him to whose six senses
you are tuned, and he to yours. Every sound matters.

Intro. Buzzes. It plays itself across your teeth, one note
stretched, metallic, ashy. East,
then its little kiltering mate, west.
Love, your arms, sleep. Your mouth stops the world.

The squawks and turnings make sense. Imagine notes echoing
back before birth. You think this could, just possibly, last.
Nothing lasts but your own gift. The air he breathes is damaged,
you resist orchestration. Your ears are fit to burst and you retreat

crooning to yourself snatches of the oldest tune left. Now the strings
cannot be disentangled, the pitch nails you underground. It happens
to the best of us, false hope, a cruel untwining. You listen too hard.
for the fridge, cars, night rustlings. Silence heals or makes mad.

Viola d'amore, your timber is a black heart. I want to hear its echo
once, the rasp of your songbird's tongue, vermillion, lento.

Revision

Love, the critic said, *is dead*. The woman
took out the blue lenses of the man's eyes.
Cold light flooded the poem.
The lovers lay pale as corpses.

Then she removed his mouth from her breast,
his hand from her wrists.
Longing, the critic said, *weakens*.
She numbed fingertips, tongue, sex.

Enough, the lover said. He pulled her down
She kissed his palm. When they dressed,
laughing like children,
his eyes were lapis, her skin rippled.

An Explanation

Words, once broadcast on mobile phones
or radio behave like light waves, they move on.
They are netted by receivers, copies are stored,
then they move again through the stellar cold.

I never said *I love you* but when you stroked
my cheek as we lay in bed in the empty house
the day I saw your unmasked face, we kissed
without desire for the first time and the last.

As you went downstairs your body aging, your face
bare, I wanted to say maybe it was love all along,
and didn't because words, once spoken
at the edge of havoc, keep travelling on through space.

The Facts

This – your solid body moving into the undertow
of the moment, says here, now is as close
to the fact as it gets. This and the sound of the door
closing. The glass paperweight on the sill is green,
a guarantee that every salt drop of me will coalesce
under your heavy shoulders, your square hands.
This drift of stolen love in the afternoon
is as close to the fact as I can bring it. Soon

your fingers bring up traces of jade, feldspar.
The body saves me. Our blue winter is over.

If they ask why in our sufficient joy we lied,
tell them we live as we can.
Say the brave look into death's eyes.
Tell them there was a war on.

The Comb

after the Irish

A small comb, lovely when it's gone
in a man's back pocket. *High up in my hair*,
She says, *is where it used to be*.
They went drinking brandy and wine, for sport.
He took his keepsake and left her owing
rowing her own boat.

Dublinia

Even those of us that never liked it,
whose capitals were Lisbon and New York,
didn't want it to come to this, the sidewalks
littered with discarded people and a spike
driven through its pot-holed heart.

Windfall

Fiddleface floated, black in the tide,
scrimwater over it. Ironwood.
He brought it ashore.
It dried out hard. Evenings
he whetted it,
wrighted it. Tight burls lightening,
shavings uncurled on the floor,
whorls unscrolled and ready
for the sweet esses carved,
the glue. He strung it.
A spring, sprang, sprung grammar of the woods
reeled out of it.
Fiddleface, long-jawed mask of a foreign crowd
sent a dark shiver around the kitchen,
sent a sound cloak
to cover two continents whirling
all from the solid block, tight
as a bard's rhyme.

Silent on the wall he calls the child:
I am the false face of your secret tribe.
Take me down. Carve a mouth.

Calypso

The moon juts her high rump over the town,
the tide rises with intent to clarify and drown.

In a dream, a boat moves over the grass.
I know her, twenty-eight foot and a mast.

The Lister engine drums like a snipe. She cuts
towards me. Two swift strokes,

Matisse blue, part the water in a V.
All I want, after the fire's hard craquelure,

is this shape, the square root of love reduced
to longing, a soft vowel held by two hard

consonants. The dreamworld insists
it is dangerous to burn away more than this.

The debris of my years is plaited into her rough tide.
I steer for the point, with its shield of stormcloud.

I will try to find, on this journey, someone
who has the recipe for honeycombs.

I leave my home – there are no companions –
and step aboard my father's boat with this instruction:

forget the stars. The cleated angle where the sky
meets to form a roof is all you can rely on now.

Two flicks of the oars and she responds, light as a wishbone,
the gods' capricious gift for this art of being alone.

The Portrait

I wasn't always like this. I learned
composure the hard way. These were not colours
I ever wore until he dressed me. I favour drabs.

It's not a likeness, more my mother or a sister.
He's elongated my face. He painted me before,
tense sharp lines, my face cut like a jewel

into a hard triangle, an unsettled dazzle of indigo,
vermilion. When he uncovered the canvas I felt
like the time I caught myself in the mirror

and it was her face. The odd thing is they never met.
It's in the bones, he said, *like disease.*
We are each other's home now, and held me all night.

There are worse lives. He calls me the companion
of his soul. Of course he cheats with models
but one of the consolations of age is a solid marriage.

He traces the notch below my throat with his thumb.
He says this is an almost perfect V. Though
I know it isn't, something stirs between my hips still.

When he paints me I see a smudge there like a bruise,
as if he wants to make his mark, a ruck
against artifice. He leaves the background dark
for our secrets. I love him well enough. He stays.

Flight

Mine is the country where men were said to die
of a woman's embrace – not of the bliss
but the brace. Where fifty-three chill women

stood tall as spears on a headland,
life in their bellies and the men dead.
Now their descendants need new blood

and a God to worship. I have been sent looking.
The way they stared dried my bones.
I left them a child, their single condition

and headed for the Albacin. There, mountains
shoulder the sky. The sea behind me is the blue
that cures. A foreigner gave me a lift. He speaks

little. Driving into the hills above Málaga
I saw his nine-fingered grip on the wheel,
his glass eye behind the shades is his ace.

There has to be a missing bit, the hook
into the unfinished world, an enticement
to the hard rage that has no healing. I won't go back.

At Erin's Dig

You are someone my family won't own
and do not visit. You get no invitation

to wedding feasts. Have you children, a husband
something to tell me? Standing at Erin's dig

beside old bones buried at a gable, the wind cuts
the planes of our faces. I think my ancestors

feared Vikings less than neighbours, that the hordes
prehistorically looting this bit of coast

were a welcome relief from long winters.
The calcination of fire scorched oysters

stopped rag and bone rotting in the midden. Blood mixed,
but the odd woman would see gold, know a moment

of love. They lived like brutes, as we do now,
without protection. They emigrated, as we did. Someone

that looked like you left his traces. You have stood
here looking out of my eyes, foreign, mistrusted.

In the portrait you are composed.
you have that look I've envied all my life

of being loved and sure of it. It's not a fake.
You earned it somehow. Why are you back?

A Stone Carver Reads Rilke

All summer the air was full of them.
His eye is drawn up into their element
as if some ocular shift enabling him to see
a new colour had occurred in June, when he read
the first Elegy, compensation for faith lost.

He is aware of birds. He buys only Italian shoes.
From that year on he gave up Christs,
Madonnas, Baby Jesuses. The angle where the marble
dovetailed into a roof no longer interested him.
He was hooked on the beginnings of terror.

Each angel is shod in hobnailed boots
weighted against her essence,
either because he trusted less
in the nature of stone than of his creation
or because he believed in stout footwear.

At Slyne Head

for Cissy

There is clearance in deep water,
the swell we know is dangerous,
is also sumptuous as it lifts always towards…
It falls back consummated and lifts away again.

It is cold, as knowledge is,
and populated by creatures indifferent
to us. Some, mysterious and huge,
lurk who knows how many fathoms down,
simple as idiots were in the medieval mind,
and just as dangerous.

The shades of our dead could be passing
below us, friendly unless proven otherwise,
their forest straight and oozing the dark green
of North, like Sibelius's *Finlandia*,
cold, separate, still and each enclosed
by a membrane, slippy as the surface of words.

The reason for this pilgrimage is clear,
to visit the chapel of our local saint
last seen with my father when I was sixteen.
Then we left the boat anchored, Aegean,
and swam in. This was before death when
all was promise – the gable's A,
a set of steps chiselled into the granite
where lightkeepers waited weeks for relief.

Reason has its place on land. Out here,
the tentative shelter of houses is nothing.
Land is where the migratory nest.
Dun Hill looks permanent but the castle
fastened to its side is sliding. It was built
on sugar slaves' backs when
people hereabouts were stained green
from famine grass about their mouths
like beasts. Such is commerce. Now, the folly
is ruined. Sugarcane Keep. Growing up,

we half expected Heathcliff, who never
turned up, so we put our faith in Grainne Mhaol
who did, centuries earlier, granted, but reliably.

Further out a slice of sea unzips,
the dolphins come choreographed,
shearing along the boat
in a slipstream. Everything lifts.
There is a moment of something so rare
it must be joy. They veer off
into the lavish swell of the west
suddenly, as if we failed to entertain.
We fish off their leavings.

The mussels' blue chainmail guards the rocks
where seals big as cattle sunbathe.
Some are in calf, a few watch from the water,
their heads pretty as models' and as sleek.
The bulls' deep bellow advises distance.

The currach is black, scale strewn,
with carpet tacked along the gunwale.
The bait rotting in a plastic barrel stinks.
I expected too much of houses –
this tarred fulcrum is home.

The island is gold with ochre lichen. It gleams.
The chapel is bare stone with an altar
and a niche high up over the entrance
arm deep, to hide the golden cup, the
manuscripts from winged marauders.
Outside, the monks' remains whiten.

I pray to the saint, genus loci because
the quivering compass
points in this direction longest. Before we picnic
and leave there is a custom to be observed.
My offering is a house key. I push it into a cleft
in the altar. It jingles down, a bright hard sound.

Suddenly the world is rimed in language
Like a skin of frost, each word minted,
my tungsten armour
my new chimed testament
to life leaving and life beginning
out of the sea, out of the sea, out of the sea.

The Black Melodeon

Is a warning hearse in Lorca's dream.
It has white New Orleans roses and a driver
out of a house of silent women.

It wails, spits, refuses to mourn.
Mostly it is silent, but its silence
has high tortoiseshell combs in its hair.

It is shuttered from the sun outside
in the hot square where a lover runs
riot with flowers in his fist.

All through this classical concerto
the black melodeon begins a poem
and each time stops just before love dies.

Outside a fountain erupts,
fingers fan over the keys, a diamond flashes,
gouts of roses scatter in the air, cold red music.

Hawk

We spotted him on Dún a Mháill,
knew him by the cloaked shoulders
and how his presence rendered
other birds unnecessary.

Beauty on the wing being this
still gaze, being alive
to his stillness as if Christlike
he had chosen us, as knowledge does.

He chased a plover close to us,
gave no slight sign that we were there
feet away in a currach,
shocked by the skill, the speed,
how he fenced space.

She feinted, pulled up sharp,
terror fuelled. Anything with a heart
would have let her go.
He fell back, vexed
and just when we thought
he'd lost her, stabbed.

Language can be like this.
A fine spray of blood
like a lacquer fan, then nothing.
Still, I want him on my wrist.